Young People From Bosnia Talk About War

Young People From Bosnia Talk About War

Harvey Fireside and Bryna J. Fireside

—Issues in Focus—

Enslow Publishers, Inc.

44 Fadem Road	PO Box 38
Box 699	Aldershot
Springfield, NJ 07081	Hants GU12 6BP
USA	UK

Library of Congress Cataloging-in Publication Data

Fireside, Harvey.
    Young people from Bosnia talk about war / Harvey Fireside and Bryna J.
Fireside.
        p. cm. — (Issues in focus)
    Includes bibliographical references and index.
    Summary: Gives a brief description of the conflict in Bosnia, including several
personal stories of tragedy told by the young people who lived through them.
    ISBN 0-89490-730-1
    1.Yugoslav War, 1991–   —Personal narratives, Bosnian—Juvenile
literature. 2. Yugoslav War, 1991–   —Children—Juvenile literature.
3. Yugoslav War, 1991 –   —Bosnia and Hercegovina—Juvenile literature.
4. Children—Bosnia and Hercegovina—Biography—Juvenile literature.
5. Bosnia and Hercegovina—History—1992–   —Juvenile literature.
[1. Yugoslav War, 1991– 2. Bosnia and Hercegovina—History.] I. Fireside,
Bryna J. II. Title. III. Series: Issues in focus (Hillside, N.J.)
DR1313.8.F57 1996
949.702'4—dc20   96-11613
                                                             CIP
                                                              AC

Printed in the United States of America

10 9 8 7 6 5 4 3 2 1

Photo Credits: Anonymous, p. 93; Bill Warren, *Ithaca (NY) Journal*
©1994, p. 33; Doug Hostetter, pp. 9, 27, 44, 53, 62, 69, 71, 82, 88;
Enslow Publishers, p. 28; Harvey Fireside, pp. 41, 84, 95; Mary Baird, p.
74; Sally Savage, p. 13.

Cover Photo: Doug Hostetter

Contents

To Tosun Bayrak and Doug Hostetter and their respective staff of many faiths who have been rescuing the youth of Bosnia.

Introduction

"To save one life, it is as if you had saved the world."
—Talmud

The Bosnian Student Project has brought just over one hundred students to study in American schools and universities since it began in 1993. Each of these students had been denied the right to continue his or her education in Bosnia because of the war there and simply because they were Muslims or children from families where there was one Muslim and one Croat or Serbian parent. The project's success is due to one simple idea, that individual people can get together and do something positive to help others.

At the beginning of the war, when Bosnian students were told to leave the University in Zagreb because the

7

Croatian government considered them to be "foreigners," a small group of students decided to organize themselves into the Association of Students of Bosnia and Herzegovina. They decided that the best way to help themselves was to stick together. As they searched for solutions to their desperate situation—no money, no place to live, no way to earn money, no way to return home—they soon found people who were willing to help them. One of these people was Professor Tosun Bayrak, who is the Sheikh (leader) of the Jerrahi Order of America, a branch of the Sufi Muslims. Professor Bayrak had traveled to Zagreb in 1993 to talk to Muslims who had no homes as a result of the war, and to see if there was anything that his congregation could do to help. When he learned of the student group, he decided that it might be possible to bring a few students to Chestnut Ridge, New York, where his mosque is located. (A mosque is a building used for public worship by Muslims.) He knew that members of his order would be happy to host the students.

It was not long before another individual, Doug Hostetter, who was then the executive director of a peace organization, the Fellowship of Reconciliation (FOR), based on nearby Nyack, New York, heard about Professor Dr. Bayrak's work. He was sure that members of his organization would also be eager to help find high schools and colleges for Bosnian students. Soon dozens of people were interested in helping.

The authors heard about the Bosnian Student Project in the winter of 1993, when only a handful of students had been brought over. It seemed like a tedious process: to find a high school or college suited to each

Sheikh Tosun Bayrak (left) and author Harvey Fireside spoke at the Jerrahi Mosque in Chestnut Ridge, New York.

student, then to have a support group raise funds for the student's transportation and living expenses. But, in the face of the spreading war in Bosnia, it was a way to do something to save lives. The only alternative was to watch the wartime destruction on television and to feel helpless to do anything about it.

To the authors, Harvey and Bryna Fireside, the story of Bosnia had a disturbingly familiar ring. Harvey Fireside had been an eight-year-old child in Vienna, Austria, in March 1938, when Hitler's armies invaded. During the two years before he and his parents came to the United States, he saw Christian neighbors—longtime friends of his family—become caught up in the Nazi measures against the Jews. Harvey was expelled from public school, his father's shop was taken over, and the family was forced to move to a district that became a Jewish ghetto. They weren't allowed to shop for food until 5:00 P.M., when the grocery shelves were nearly bare. He remembers bringing a pot to a soup kitchen set up by private relief organizations, to get the one hot meal of the day.

Finally, relatives in Illinois sent Harvey and his parents an "affidavit of support" to guarantee that as new immigrants to the United States they would not need welfare from the government. Before they could leave Vienna, however, they had to go through lots of red tape. When Harvey read about "ethnic cleansing" of Bosnian Muslims by Serbian troops, it brought back memories of the districts of Vienna that were declared *judenrein*—cleansed of Jews.

Bryna Fireside had grown up in a Jewish family in New Jersey, aware that distant relatives in Poland and

Lithuania were being murdered by the Nazis during World War II. Later, she learned that the Western governments, including her own, were aware of what became known as the Holocaust, but did relatively little to stop it. It was far more likely for survivors to be saved through the actions of private individuals or rescue groups. Her grandparents helped the only surviving two cousins in her family from Poland come to the United States after the war.

Harvey and Bryna Fireside have observed the growth of the Bosnian Student Project in their hometown, Ithaca, New York, in the last two years. It began with the arrival of one student in February 1993, when a small group of about a dozen men and women formed a support network. By 1996, there were about thirty people who met regularly with five Bosnian students each month—and the list of those who contribute to the support of the students was up to 150. In addition to the five students who are currently studying at Cornell University and Tompkins Cortland Community College, the group has helped to bring four more students to nearby college towns.

The group membership includes Jews, Muslims, Protestants, and Catholics who share equally in the joy of their students' achievements and who offer the students friendship, driving lessons, shared dinners, tutoring, and medical and legal services.

At first, some of the new arrivals from Bosnia were reluctant to accept invitations from community groups to talk about their wartime experiences. With encouragement from their sponsors, however, the students agreed to speak to local schools, clubs, churches, and synagogues. They found that the sympathy from their listeners helped them to begin to heal the wounds of war and, eventually, to overcome their private nightmares. They also discovered that speaking about these experiences helped to educate Americans about Bosnia, and to show them, by example, that young Bosnians shared the appearance and cultural values of many Americans.

The authors saw the mutual benefit of these exchanges, so they asked FOR to help them arrange interviews from a larger sample of Bosnian students. With Doug Hostetter's help, they conducted twenty-five interviews in the winter of 1994 and spring of 1995. They found students from all parts of Bosnia who volunteered to tell their stories in English, except for two who spoke through an interpreter. The students were interviewed in Ithaca, New York, at the FOR offices in Nyack, New York, at the mosque of the Jerrahi Order of America in Chestnut Ridge, New York, and over Christmas break 1994 at their reunion held at the Quaker conference center in Pendle Hill, Pennsylvania.

As of November 1995, 109 high school and college students had come to study in the United States through the Bosnian Student Project. Sixty-six colleges and universities have provided scholarships for the college students. But there are still many excellent students who are waiting for a call from FOR with the news that another person has found a college willing to offer scholarship aid—and that there are a few good people who will provide a home and financial support to help the students through a difficult adjustment period.

Doug Hostetter (seated), director of the Bosnian Student Project, talked with one of the Bosnian students in his office at the Fellowship of Reconciliation in Nyack, New York.

Even though it is not possible for one person to save the world, it is possible for one individual to save one other individual during wartime.

The authors hope that you will be left not with impressions of cruelty by the persecutors of these students, but with an appreciation of the kindness that enabled the students to survive and bring the spirit of tolerance and forgiveness to the task of rebuilding Bosnia and their lives.

1

Roots of War

There are at least three different ways to view the conflict that has resulted in the destruction of Bosnia since spring 1992: through Muslim, Croatian, or Serbian eyes. The Muslims see themselves as having been attacked by their two more powerful neighbors. For merely declaring their independence from Bosnia, they have been driven out of scores of towns, where their religious and cultural centers (mosques, libraries, and museums) were destroyed. They have suffered nearly two hundred thousand casualties—one tenth of their people. Thousands of women have been raped, and more than a million Muslims have been forced to become refugees.[1] While thousands of Serbs and Croats were also forced to flee, they had homelands that offered them refuge, but the Bosnian Muslims have nowhere to go. And their suffering has not brought much help from the governments of Western Europe or the United States.

The Croatians see themselves as a thriving northern republic of Yugoslavia, composed of hard-working people who believe in a free market (with businesses run by individuals, not the government). They resent having been forced to pay more than their fair share of Yugoslavia's budget in the 1970s and 1980s. They felt threatened by the claims of Serbian leaders, whom they regarded as still practicing an outdated form of communism.[2] They saw their smaller neighbor, Slovenia, preparing to become independent on June 26, 1991, making it a good time for Croats to go their own way as well, in the face of Serbian hostility. They were eager to claim a share of Bosnia's territory to the west and south. But they underestimated the fears of their own Serbian minority.

In 1990, the Serbian population of Croatia, alerted by three years of dire warnings by Serbian president Slobodan Milosevic (Slo-BO-dahn Me-LO-she-vitch), felt certain that the election of Franjo Tudjman (FRAN-yo TOOJ-mahn) as Croatian president would lead to cycles of roundups and killings. The Serbs recalled their suffering during World War II, when the fascist government of Croatia, known as the Ustasha, had murdered thousands of their countrymen. In Tudjman's words and symbols, they saw a revival of the Ustasha campaign of hatred against the Serbs.

The Serbian attack on Croatia in mid-1991 served as a dress rehearsal for the invasion of Bosnia in the following spring. Extreme nationalists (people with an exaggerated sense of devotion to their land) had come to

Croatia from Belgrade, the Serbian capital, to organize armed resistance by local Serbs to any attack.

In May 1991, an incident seems to have set off the Croat-Serbian war. There are sharply differing accounts from each side, but it appears that Serbs in the village of Borovo Selo had set up a roadblock to prevent Croatian militia from patrolling the area. They held two police officers hostage; twenty more members of the militia came to rescue them, then still other reinforcements arrived, and a firefight began. By the time the smoke cleared, about seventeen of the combatants (the numbers vary in the reports) lay dead.[3] For Milosevic, the Serbian president, this was the reason to declare war on Croatia, a conflict that would result in over twenty thousand casualties.

The war began with Serbian attacks on two civilian centers, first a four-month siege of Vukovar (VOO-ko-var) which totally destroyed that city founded in the Middle Ages, then an attack on Dubrovnik (DOO-brov-nick), known as "the Pearl of the Adriatic," an ancient cultural center and resort, that lacked any evident military value. The exile or murder of the Croats who defended these cities and the widespread looting by Serb "irregular forces" aroused worldwide sympathy for Croatia and criticism of Serbia. (To be fair, it should be mentioned that Croatian attacks on Serbian villages, which sent fifty thousand people fleeing as refugees, did not get the same coverage abroad.)[4] Tudjman's Croatian government was recognized internationally in December 1991.

This conflict, which officially came to an end with the signing of a 1995 peace accord, had a number of consequences. It showed the Serbian leaders that they would need supply lines through Bosnia to reach their countrymen in Croatia. As their main forces began to withdraw from Croatia, they began to make preparations for the next war, against the Bosnian Muslims.

The United Nations criticized the Serbian invasion, and the Serbs felt backed into a corner by international peacekeeping forces. An arms embargo ordered UN member states not to send weapons to the former Yugoslavia; it was followed by economic sanctions—a ban on major trade items—against Serbia. Only the Russian government maintained an attitude of traditional friendship with the Serbs. After all, they are fellow Slavs with whom Russians share a religious tradition and a system of writing. President Milosevic's group tightened its control over newspapers and television in Serbia. The media spread his message that Serbia was righting ancient wrongs and fighting for its survival while surrounded by enemies at home and abroad.[5]

Nearly four years of war in Bosnia were officially brought to an end with the signing of a peace agreement by all sides in November 1995. But only time will tell if real peace will result.

In this republic (roughly the size of Oregon) in the center of the country that used to be Yugoslavia, there were three warring armies: the Serbian forces, the Croatian army, and the Muslim troops. The Serbians were the best equipped, made up of members of the old Yugoslav army (fifth strongest in Europe) and of local Serb forces. With hundreds of tanks, fighter planes, attack helicopters, and guns, the Serbians were able to occupy about 70 percent of Bosnia by mid-1992, although Serbs form only 31 percent of Bosnia's original population.[6] Croatian troops took over about 20 percent of Bosnian territory along their joint border, where there is a cluster of Croatian people, who make up 17 percent of the republic's population.[7]

Caught between these two armies, the Muslims (44 percent of the population) were squeezed into cities and villages in central and eastern Bosnia. Their capital of Sarajevo and other urban centers were surrounded by Serbian troops, generally on hillsides from which they were firing artillery shells at will on the houses below. Of the three armies, the Muslims were the least prepared for the war. Muslim army veterans and local forces, with outdated rifles, were quickly organized to defend the government that declared Bosnia's independence in March 1992. The next month the government of Bosnia was under attack.[8]

We will not attempt to give a full account of the complicated history of Yugoslavia in this brief chapter. At best, we can try to present the reasons given by the groups that have been fighting in Bosnia. What we have learned from interviewing the students is that the groups see each other as sworn enemies in a fight for survival. These extreme views are more a reflection of stereotypes than representative of the way real people act.

None of the two dozen Bosnian students we have interviewed, however, hate all of the Serbs or the Croats whose troops pushed them out of their homes. They explain that most members of the opposing groups are good people, who will help each other as individuals. But when leaders use the media to show each group fighting against its "enemies," a lifetime of goodwill can be replaced by anger.

One of the stereotypes we found false is the idea that Muslims look or behave differently from Serbs or Croats. Indeed, they look and act very much alike. The history of the country indicates that all three groups—Muslims, Croats, and Serbs—were originally from the same country that came to call itself Yugoslavia, or "south Slavia."

In the fourteenth century, the Ottoman Turks, who were Muslims, conquered the southern half of the country, where most of the Christian Serbs lived. The Serb warriors, led by Prince Lazar, were defeated by Ottoman troops on June 28, 1389, at Kosovo Polje (KOS-o-vo POL-ye)—the "field of blackbirds." That date and place have become enshrined as holy in the history of Serbia.[9] The historic battle marks the beginning of about four hundred years of Ottoman domination of the Serbs, who worked as servants and paid heavy taxes. Thousands of them—the ancestors of today's Bosnians—chose to convert to Islam. When they did so, the Turks allowed them to become landowners and to move into the ruling class.[10] Six hundred years later, the Serbs, who practice an Eastern Orthodox form of Christianity, still have not forgiven the Bosnian Muslims and call them, disparagingly, "Turks."

Within the territory of Bosnia is a group of Serbians who some four hundred years ago were invited by Austria to become a frontier military force. (The Serbo-Croatian word for border is Krajina (CRY-ee-nah). This is important today because Krajina Serbs have been the fiercest fighters in the conflict. They refused to recognize the government of Bosnia, with its Muslim president. And they set up their own mini-state, with its own capital.

The leader of these Serbs, Dr. Radovan Karadzic (RAH-do-VAHN KA-ra-TITCH), claimed that the "Muslim state" of Bosnia, under President Alija Izetbegovic (AH-lee-ya Ee-zet-BEG-o-vitch), would be a threat to the Christian life of his people.[11] The Bosnian government, in turn, feared that the Serbians would expel remaining Muslims from their homes and wipe out their culture. The Bosnian leaders said they wanted to share power in the government among the three religious and ethnic groups, to salvage a truly multicultural society.

In effect, neither side trusted the other. The Americans and West Europeans tried to settle the conflict. They came up with various plans to split up the country—either into three substates, for the three major ethnic groups: Muslims, Croats, and Serbs, or into a checkerboard of ten ethnic territories.[12]

Basically, the major governments—Croatia, Bosnia, and Serbia—have accepted this partition plan, at least as the framework for discussion while the fighting stops. While this book was being written, the United States held a peace conference that guaranteed the continued existence of Bosnia. The Krajina Serbs, however, fear that the Croats and Bosnians will team up against them. They resent the fact that their president, Radovan Karadzic, and some of their military commanders have been indicted as "war criminals" by the International Court of Justice at the Hague. Thus, they cannot attend a peace conference abroad without the risk of being arrested, and have to let Serbian president Milosevic represent them.

Milosevic built his political career on being an outspoken nationalist, but he is now trying to be a "peacemaker." On June 28, 1989, he gave a speech at Kosovo Polje to celebrate the six hundredth anniversary of Prince Lazar's defeat. He said, "They'll never do this to you again. Never again will anyone defeat you."[13] His words won Milosevic first the Communist party leadership, then the presidency of Serbia by a landslide in elections held in December 1990. His platform called for a defense of the Serbians who lived in Bosnia and Croatia, leading to a "Greater Serbia" that occupies more and more of its neighbors' lands.[14]

Like the Serbs, the Croats were also pulled along the road to ever more extreme nationalist politics. The result of their elections in April 1990 was to install a hard-line president, Franjo Tudjman, a historian and a former general in the Yugoslav army, who began to build up a Croat military force independent of the Serb-dominated national army. Despite the growing tension between these two powers, presidents Milosevic and Tudjman held a series of meetings in March 1991. Trying to prevent a possible war between their countries, they agreed on the future division of Bosnia.[15] The country's control has been split between the three. Muslims control about 25 percent, Croats control another 25 percent, and the remaining 50 percent is under Serb control.

The war between Croatia and Serbia left the leaders of Bosnia facing a decision: They could side with either of their powerful neighbors and risk being swallowed up, or they could follow Croatia's example and opt for independence.[16] In truth, they lacked the military force to defend themselves, but they wanted to follow the example of other formerly Communist countries by breaking up into separate ethnic states. The Bosnians thought they could also expect foreign recognition of their independence. They would soon find out, however, that Western powers were ready with words but not actions to make Bosnian "self-determination" a reality.

The Bosnian government overestimated Western support and underestimated the degree of hostility from its native Serbian minority to splitting off from Yugoslavia. This may have been due to a false sense of security born in the era of united Yugoslavia's longtime leader, Josip Broz, better known as Marshal Tito. Who could be blamed for thinking that the peace that had prevailed following World War II under Tito's slogan "Unity and Brotherhood" would continue?

Tito's method of stopping the traditional ethnic rivalries among Croats, Serbs, and Muslims was to make all expressions of nationalism—the desire for separate states based on nationality—illegal. Instead of saying that they were Serbians or Croatians, for example, all the people were supposed to think of themselves as simply belonging to a common Yugoslav nation. Although this seemed to have worked for about forty-five years, it now appears that Tito merely put the lid on a pressure cooker that was due to explode after his death.

From the student interviews, we learned that Muslim families looked back fondly on the Tito era, as a time of growing prosperity, when Yugoslavia was the most Westernized of the Communist countries, with free education and health care, a spirit of tolerance among various ethnic and religious groups, and hope for the future. In fact, there was a great spirit of tolerance, because about one in four Yugoslavs intermarried.

In the 1970s, however, the last decade of Tito's life, there were some dark clouds on the horizon: The big sums of money Yugoslavia had borrowed abroad caused a high inflation rate which undermined the economy. There was a widening gap between the wealthy northern parts of the country and the poor southern areas. And in 1974 a decentralized government gave each of the republics veto power over central decisions.[17]

By loosening the national controls from the Yugoslav capital, Belgrade, Tito allowed the political bosses of each republic to follow his own showy lifestyle, with his dozens of luxurious vacation homes. These bosses created wasteful programs of building roads and factories without considering what might be best for the entire country.[18]

It seems ironic that the Tito system was able to employ a dictatorship to keep the peace for forty-five years. However, a mere decade after his death in 1980, the turn to democracy, with free elections in 1990—the first in more than sixty years—soon led to bitter ethnic warfare.

The causes for the collapse of "Titoism" were many. Inside Yugoslavia, there was no person of Tito's stature to keep the Serbs and Croats in line after his death. The ethnic leaders who won the elections brought up the old hatreds and put people in a position to fight against their neighbors.

However, what happened to Yugoslavia was also linked to the rest of Eastern Europe and the Soviet Union. For in 1989–1990, the Berlin Wall came down, and the Communist governments that had ruled the six countries of Eastern Europe lost their power.[19] Mikhail Gorbachev, the Soviet president, tried hard—but it turned out, unsuccessfully—to hold his country together, as the various "union republics" (the Baltic states, Ukraine, Georgia, and others) began campaigns to split off from Russia. In all of these countries, the governments were based on communism and Communist leaders claimed to have overcome old ethnic loyalties by uniting members of the working class against their oppressors.[20]

Communism was supposed to have changed human nature, to root out selfishness, and to promote pursuit of the common good. But even in Russia, after more than seventy years of Soviet rule, it appeared that when the authorities were unable to maintain central control, the people went back to their old ways, including restoration of the right to private property and separatist republics.

In Yugoslavia, too, fragile national patriotism quickly yielded to the ethnic loyalties of pre-Communist days. And there, in a more open and widespread way than elsewhere in Eastern Europe, that meant engaging in bitter warfare, with no end in sight.

So far, we have reviewed some of the reasons given for the violence:

1. Today's Serbs, Croats, and Muslims fought over a history that divided them for six hundred years.

2. More recent causes for bitterness stem from the groups in Yugoslavia that fought so fiercely against each other and with the Nazi troops that occupied their country during World War II.

3. The Serbians planned to take over much of Bosnia as the only way of securely linking their scattered settlements in the Krajina.

4. Tito's attempt to build a new Yugoslav nation could not outlive him because his successors wanted to lead separate mini-states instead.

These reasons for the war in Bosnia are accepted, more or less, by scholars and governments in the West. However, while each of these explanations contains truth, they do not really tell us why the war continued without ceasing, even three years after Serbia and Croatia reached their announced objectives. Every month (until the peace treaty of November 1995), new scenes of death and destruction appeared on television. Is it possible that the official Western view—seeing the Bosnian conflict as essentially a civil war, based on century-old grudges—is popular because it excuses the governments of Europe and the United States, even the United Nations (UN), for doing so little to bring peace? The UN has sent in "observers," but these troops avoid being involved. Indeed, they were replaced by NATO (United States and European) units under the November 1995 peace agreement.

The Western air of detachment until late 1995 depended on seeing the Bosnian war as somehow not real and discounting the images on our television sets. The stories that the students told us are reminders that we are not talking about abstract forces of history but about real people who decided to go to war against their neighbors. Their leaders may have told them that they were righting "ancient wrongs," but often such noble words were an excuse to take over a neighbor's house and his possessions, to chase away those with a different religion or nationality—and even to kill them.

Most of the students have mixed feelings about the peace accords that the leaders of Serbia, Croatia, and Muslim Bosnia signed at a conference arranged by the United States in Dayton, Ohio, in November 1995. They are happy that all the warring factions agreed to stop fighting and to let United States and other NATO troops, plus a small Russian unit, set up corridors of peacekeepers between the armies. The students are

This bombed-out school building in Krupa is a reminder of the death and destruction that the war in Bosnia has caused.

27

This map shows the divisions to the former Yugoslavia. Surrounding countries are also shown.

unhappy that, after four years of fighting in their homeland, Bosnia has been divided: half to be occupied by Serbs, the other half by a federation of Muslims and Croats. The students had hoped to be free to return to their hometowns. While the accords do provide for the return of refugees, some of these places have been destroyed, others ended up in control of hostile groups that won't let the original inhabitants back. Finally, the students had hoped to come home to a multi-ethnic Bosnia—where Muslims, Croats, and Serbs could live together in harmony. While that is the status of the Bosnian capital, Sarajevo, under the accord, there are still Serbs who refuse to accept the Muslim-run city government occupying some of the suburbs.

The peace accords provide for elections in all parts of Bosnia to form a common government by autumn 1996. The students doubt that this political settlement will really occur. They are also afraid that renewed fighting will break out after the peacekeepers leave. Still, they hope it will be safe for them to return eventually, and to apply the skills they have acquired to repair the wartime destruction. They insist that they do not hate any other group—although they would like to see the worst war criminals on each side tried and punished. They grew up with friendships that bridged religious and ethnic lines. They now look forward to a new phase in the history of their country, when neighbors can again greet each other as fellow human beings with equal rights respected by all.

2

Arriving in the United States: Maja's Story

Maja* stared out of the bus window on the chilly afternoon of February 4, 1994, wondering what awaited her in Ithaca, a town in upstate New York.[1] "I was a little bit scared because I didn't know what to expect," she said. "I was really suspicious after everything that happened to me." Still, she was thrilled to have the chance to become a student again. She hoped to use her education to help people back in her war-torn country, but for months—maybe years—she would have to be on her own, separated from her family. Her parents were not eligible for refugee visas to come to the United States because they had managed to get to Turkey and were not "in immediate danger."

* Not her real name.

Maja's journey had taken her thousands of miles from her home in Sarajevo, the capital of Bosnia, an ancient city at the center of the country that used to be Yugoslavia. She had received a message from Doug Hostetter, the international secretary for a peace group called the Fellowship of Reconciliation (FOR). He told her about a group of people in Ithaca, New York, who had not only found a scholarship for her to a nearby community college but also promised to support her while she went to school.

"At first, I thought, 'Why would strangers help me if they don't want anything from me?'"

What Maja didn't yet know was that there were about two dozen people in Ithaca—Jews, Christians, and Muslims—who went into action the moment they learned there was a way to help a Bosnian student.

Raquib Zaman, a business professor from Bangladesh, said, "Our Muslim community had heard about the suffering in Bosnia. We were happy to join an interfaith group to support Maja."

Sandy Pollock, an English teacher, called Dr. Eduardo Marti, president of the Tompkins Cortland Community College (TC-3), to explain Maja's situation. Marti immediately agreed to offer her free tuition, as long as she was a qualified student. Once Maja sent her high school and university records to TC-3, there was no doubt that she would be an excellent student. Her grades from the University of Sarajevo, where she had completed one year, were all 1s and 2s ("A"s and "B"s). She was sent the papers that entitled her to apply for a student visa at the American embassy in Istanbul. Her airfare to New York was paid for by FOR and a Muslim group, the Jerrahi Order of America.

"I didn't have a clue who the Jerrahis were," said Maja. She was worried that they would not welcome her since she was only half-Muslim and definitely not religious.

She was met at Kennedy Airport by Doug Hostetter and taken to spend the night with a family in Nyack, New York. Doug reassured her that neither the Jerrahis nor anyone else was concerned about her religious practices. On Friday at noon, she boarded the bus to Ithaca with her one suitcase.

Maja's sponsors had been busy. Brenda Wallace, the woman who managed the bus station, ordered a dozen roses to welcome her. A reporter from the *Ithaca Journal*, the local newspaper, came with a photographer to capture Maja's first moments in town. A camera crew from the television station was also on hand, as was the chairman of the county government, Dr. Marti, and about twenty members of the newly formed Bosnian Student Project. When Maja stepped off the bus she saw a crowd of people waiting for her, holding up banners welcoming her in English and in her native language, Serbo-Croatian. Rabbi Larry Edwards, Jewish Chaplain at Cornell University, handed her a bouquet of flowers and a check for her immediate expenses.

"I was shocked," she said. "I didn't expect it would be like that. I didn't know I was so important. The only thing that mattered to me was the opportunity to study and get my education."

The first words Maja heard in Ithaca were in her own language. Wayles Browne, a professor of languages

Maja responded with surprise and happiness after a fourteen-hour plane trip from Istanbul to New York City, and a five-hour bus ride from New York City to Ithaca, New York, on a cold February evening. She was greeted by a welcoming committee that included the president of Tompkins Cortland Community College and many well-wishers.

welcomed her first in Serbo-Croatian, then in English. He told her that she would stay with him and his wife for the first few weeks.

Dr. Marti said how honored he was to have her as a student. He himself was once a refugee who had come to the United States as a young boy from Cuba. "I, too, came by myself to a strange land, with strange people," he said. "My English was very similar to hers. The horrors of war and revolution don't go away with time. I feel a certain kinship with Maja."

"I was happy to see the group that met me—Christians, Jews, and Muslims. It gave me hope," Maja recalled.

But after two days of travel with very little sleep, she found she could barely eat dinner at the restaurant to which she was taken by her host family and two of her other sponsors.

Maja's hosts were ordinary people, ready to help her simply because it seemed like the right thing to do. They were pleasantly surprised to find that the young woman looked just like the students attending Cornell University or Ithaca College. She was wearing stylish clothes: jeans, a ski jacket, leather boots. Her reddish hair and her makeup didn't fit their idea of a Muslim, like the ones from the Middle East. Maja was European, and her middle-class family had brought her up in a Western urban lifestyle. She was familiar with television, the latest rock groups, and American movies.

When Maja spoke, her English sounded awkward but it could be understood. "I want first to clear up any misunderstanding," she said. "You invited me as a Muslim, but I am really only half-Muslim and half-Christian, like maybe a third of the Sarajevo population. Doesn't that matter to you?"

"Not at all," answered Joey Cardamone, a high-school teacher. "You are welcome regardless of your nationality or religion. We just want to help students whose lives have been disrupted by the war. You are certainly qualified, as a refugee from Bosnia and Turkey." Cardamone knew that Maja's father was still suffering the aftereffects of torture in prison and that her mother was unable to resume her teaching career as a Christian in Istanbul.

Raquib Zaman wanted to know what Maja really wanted to study. She explained that her original major at the University of Sarajevo had been business, in the School of Economics. In Europe, students decide from their first day in college what their career plans are. In the United States, however, many students don't decide on a major area of study for a year or two, and they take many general courses in the liberal arts. Since her father was the manager of a bus company, and had even helped to organize transportation for the athletes who had come to Sarajevo for the 1984 Winter Olympics, Maja had thought international business would be exciting for her, too.

"Lately," she said, "I think it might actually be a better idea to study psychology. Then I would be ready to return to Bosnia prepared for the many people who will need help adjusting to normal life after the war is over." Maja could see herself as a psychologist, or a social worker, or even a doctor. But first she knew she had to learn how to express herself better in English.

Her sponsors told Maja that there was no need to make a career choice for a while. They had arranged for her to be given tests at TC-3 on Monday morning. An adviser would tell her about the available programs after her tests were scored. If she did well in her semester at that college, she would be able to apply for admission and financial aid at a four-year school. If she preferred, however, she could stay at the community college for a two-year degree.

By this time, Maja was quite exhausted. She was taken to the Browne house—still smiling, though. It was difficult for her to go to sleep. "I was in a strange room," she said later, "staring at the ceiling and crying, until my ears were full of tears."

On Monday, however, Maja was ready at 8 A.M. to be taken to the school. She was worried about starting school nearly three weeks after it began, but again she was surprised by how warmly people welcomed her. She was told that there would be a chance for her to catch up. "They were so friendly and helpful and so encouraging at TC-3," she recalled. "The first couple of days I was really scared. But they convinced me that nothing bad would happen to me. They were so kind and gentle."

In the next few weeks, Maja learned to take the bus to TC-3 every other day. It was a half-hour ride, and there were always friendly greetings from students and teachers waiting for her. Many people recognized her from the stories in the newspaper and on television. She met the people who were supporting her and was astounded to see how many had volunteered to help her. A doctor and a dentist offered their services. An attorney offered her his office phone to call her parents and sister any time. The Bosnian Student Project gave her money for textbooks, bus fares, and any other small items she might need.

After the newspaper story about her arrival appeared, thirteen people called the committee to offer her a place to live. She had dinner with Cathy Martin*, a social worker and therapist. "I met her children," Maja remembered. "It was a beautiful place, and she is a wonderful person. She became a special friend." They agreed it was the perfect place for her to stay. In her many talks with Cathy, Maja could open up about the horrible experiences she had lived through. For example, when she played with Cathy's big black cat, she could recall how terrified she had been when Serbian soldiers had arrested her father.

"The ones who abducted him were maybe twenty years old," her mother told her.

"They kept telling him that he must have lots of money," she said. They wanted to take it from him, even though he gave them all the money he had in the apartment and said there were no millions of dollars there. But what stuck in her mind, she said, was that her two Siamese cats got their backs up and were hissing at the soldiers.

Maja found it very painful to bring back the memories of her peaceful world that was shattered overnight. "To me, Sarajevo is the most beautiful place in the world," she said. "The image of that place, the spirit of that people, our lifestyle." What made it special for her was that she could feel like a citizen of the larger country, Yugoslavia, rather than part Muslim, part Serb.

---

* Not her real name.

"Bosnia was really mixed," she explained. It was home to Serbians, Croats, Muslims, and Jews. The logo on the Sarajevo television was a picture of the city's main square, with a mosque for Muslims, a synagogue for Jews, and a cathedral for Christians. "Everybody lived there a thousand years together."

The question she keeps asking herself is, "How did those people, our neighbors, become such animals and lunatics?" How could they forget their friendships so quickly and turn into deadly enemies? The people of Sarajevo had watched the fighting break out in other parts of Yugoslavia, but it seemed far away. "We were saying, 'No, no. It can't happen here. No, this is different. People in Sarajevo are reasonable. We are different.'"

Maja's father, a Muslim, was not religious. Her mother, a Christian Serb, was a high-school science teacher, and very open-minded. Maja was used to living in a mixed ethnic neighborhood in Sarajevo, and having friends of all religions and nationalities. Then, in April 1992, some neighborhood teenagers showed up in Serbian army uniforms. "Just overnight the neighbors became soldiers," she said. "They seized my father's car and after they bombed his bus depot he couldn't work any longer."

Stores were being looted, and it wasn't safe to be outside because of sniper fire. Maja's parents thought it best to send their two daughters to her mother's relatives in Belgrade, the capital of Serbia.

As Maja told the story of her flight from Sarajevo, it is clear that, in the midst of all the remembered fear and suffering, she feels a deep admiration for her parents. They are good, decent people, who began to feel helpless in the face of growing lawlessness. But their courage set an example for Maja and her younger sister, Rodina*.

As she later learned from her mother, the soldiers had kidnapped her father. They had come back a second time to demand all valuables and a million dollars from her mother. "I gave them all our jewelry and gold, silverware and the paintings," her mother said. When they wanted the wedding ring she had worn for twenty-five years, however, she refused. When nothing more was heard from her father, the mother "was really crazy with fear. She thought they were going to kill him. . . . Then she calmed down and called a doctor." This was a Serbian family friend, forced to become an officer in the Yugoslav army. He said, "I will look in every concentration camp for him."

Meanwhile, Maja's father had been repeatedly beaten by the soldiers. His ribs were broken and he had trouble breathing. They kept him barely alive so that he could order the million-dollar ransom they thought he must be hiding somewhere. When he was thrown in with a roomful of corpses, he refused to be humiliated any longer. "Why don't you just kill me?" he asked them, wanting to end his suffering. But, to his surprise, he later told Maja, "they began laughing. And they didn't hit me any more."

Eventually, the family friend discovered Maja's father near death at a prison camp. As a high-ranking officer, he was able to order the father's release into his custody and to find him emergency care at a Serbian army hospital. To continue the treatment, doctors

---

* Not her real name.

ordered him flown to a clinic in Belgrade, where his daughters finally located him. They were shocked. "He was black from the beatings and his mouth was bloody. We tried to hug him, but he said no, he was in such pain. He said, 'You know, the only thing that kept me alive was the knowledge that you two were so young and I still have to take care of you.'"

Maja's mother—along with all the other residents of her apartment house—was forced to leave all her possessions except for what she could squeeze into a small suitcase and to board a bus. The soldiers were debating whether or not to shoot these people or to take them to a concentration camp. At last, they decided to unload them at a bridge leading to the Muslim section of Sarajevo. There Maja's mother learned that her husband and daughters had been allowed to join a cousin in Istanbul, Turkey. Hard as it was to leave her native city, the mother decided that her place was with them. When she got to Turkey, however, she found that, as a Christian, she was made to feel very unwelcome. Though Maja's mother is only in her late forties, Maja says her brown hair "has turned all white. And since she is considered a 'guest' in Turkey, she is unable to work," while her father's physical condition allows him to work only a few hours a week. Recently, however, Maja's father received a work permit.

Still, Maja finds her parents are happy that she is finally in the United States. Out of gratitude to the people taking care of her, "my parents are helping children without parents."

In September 1994, the Bosnian Student Project was able to bring Maja's sister Rodina to join Maja in Ithaca.

Maja (left) and her sister, Rodina, were reunited at the bus station in Ithaca, New York, after being separated for eight months.

Rodina is now a student at TC-3. The two girls speak to their parents regularly by phone, thanks to Ray Schlather, the attorney who has given them an unlimited number of calls home.

Both sisters have overcome their fears about telling their story to American audiences. It is their way of keeping alive a city that lives on in their memory. Maja isn't sure she can ever accept the destruction that has come to Sarajevo. "I know," she said, "that city parks and football stadiums became cemeteries because people had no places to make normal graveyards." Some day, she hopes, it will be possible for her family to return and to help heal the wounds of a brutal war.

3

Good Neighbors
Become Enemies

One of the most puzzling episodes in their lives, according to the Bosnian students now in the United States, was how a lifetime of being accepted as Muslims among Serbs and Croatians turned into the present period of mutual suspicion and hatred. They kept wondering: Had the Serb attack on Muslims been planned secretly for a long time? Why didn't the friends they had grown up with defend them? Could the bitterness ever be overcome?

Emir

"We lived happily until the war started," recalled Emir, an eighteen-year-old with horn-rimmed glasses.[1] He is a

Emir's life was changed forever by the approach of the Yugoslav army into his hometown of Prijedor, Bosnia, in 1992. He is now studying American literature at Evergreen College in Washington State, and hopes to become a professor.

student of American literature at Evergreen College in Washington State. With a thick book of poetry under his arm, Emir already looks a bit like the professor he wants to become.

The Muslims in Emir's hometown, Prijedor (Pree-YAY-dor), "did not really see it coming," he said. "It was closing in on everybody, but we didn't want to believe the prospect. It appeared with great swiftness. We found ourselves pretty much taken by surprise."

Emir's young life was divided in two by the approach of the Yugoslav army into northwest Bosnia in April 1992. Before that, he said, "my childhood was a happy one. [I was] an only son of rather influential parents. I had everything I wanted. The problem was only what to want." Afterwards, everything the family owned was gone. As he said, "All my books and all our family photographs are buried somewhere near my house. That is where my past lies."

It doesn't seem that the possessions he had to leave behind matter the most to Emir. His family had plenty of material things—and he knew that, even if most of them were gone, they could eventually be replaced. Except, of course, the family photos—pictures of a happier time—that stand for his "past." What hurt him the most, however, he explained, is that he had grown up trusting his friends and neighbors, and now he felt hurt by them.

"My family knew a great number of people," he said, "and a lot of their friends really turned into enemies; however, some of our Serbian friends did not turn against us. Unfortunately, the good ones are [all too often] the exception.

"It amazed me when my mother would tell me that a person who used to have lunch with my father every day said that he ought to be shot." His father's "crime," according to Emir, was that—as a social worker—he was considered "an intellectual," somebody to be treated with suspicion. Further, his father had been "politically involved," and "he was sort of prominent."

Emir's mother was also a professional, a doctor in the local hospital. She soon became aware that her colleagues were beginning to treat Muslim physicians as enemies of the people. "Every day," Emir recalled, "the Serbian radio and TV gave out this propaganda. They said that this very well-know Muslim doctor had castrated Serbian children at birth. . . . They accused him of having done this for ten years. My mother told us her Serbian doctor friends had said he was a beast. And my mother said that the story was a lie, and quite impossible. But people really believed it."

If Muslims were depicted as evil and dangerous, Emir said, it was easier for Serbian forces to launch an attack on them. "That, plus the gains you could get from robbing your neighbors—I think that was pretty much enough to make people do atrocious things."

Emir believes that middle-class Muslims were an object of envy for their Serb and Croat neighbors. "Greed was a big part of it—lust after people's goods. Robbery was the most frequent crime committed in this war. Everybody's possessions were robbed—all the money they could find."

Much of the Muslim population of Prijedor was forced to leave town, as part of the Serbs' "ethnic cleansing." During their transport in cattle trucks, they were

46

terrorized into giving up all their valuables. "After twenty kilometers, they got to the first checkpoint. They took one man from the truck and beat him severely; then they would give him a cloth bag to collect all the 'Serbian money,' so they could say no Serbians were involved.

"The next checkpoint came, and they took the same person and beat him again and said, 'Now the Deutschmarks.' And then other currency, then jewelry, and watches. By then people gave up everything, for fear of being searched and killed. At the end, if [the Serbs] found any valuables on anyone he would be killed."

Emir showed little emotion when he recalled, "All of our possessions were taken. It was normal practice. It was unusual when someone was able to save something. At first I felt bad, but now I forget. I hardly remember what I had. My parents are alive, and that makes up for it."

Emir sees the fact that he and his parents survived as a "fortunate thing." "My parents decided to send me out before it was too late, and I went to Zagreb to stay with my grandparents. My grandfather died just the day I got there, so my father drove me to the funeral. While that seemed to be a misfortune, it brought about a pretty good thing. When we arrived, the bridge that connected Bosnia and Croatia was cut off. My father couldn't go back—and that saved his life. He would have been killed" if he had gone back to Prijedor.

Emir's mother "was in less danger of being killed because she was alone. She stayed for a couple of months until she was expelled by the Serbs. Though we lost everything we had, she managed to get out alive. This was a great thing. Fifty to 60 percent of the people I knew are dead or missing."

Emir's parents were reunited in August 1992. But they "left to go to Germany as refugees because of the insecurity of life in Zagreb." Emir stayed behind with his relatives, to complete his first year of high school. "I spoke some English. I learned English in a foreign language program, but then I didn't speak a word for two years." Then he was introduced to Dr. Tosun Bayrak, the leader of the Jerrahi Order of America, who "asked me to translate something—and it came back to me."

It was what Emir calls his "affinity toward English" that led to his being chosen as the first Bosnian student whom the Jerrahis brought to the United States. To finish high school, he was "placed with a regular family—mom and dad and two children. The family was very good to me, and that made my adjustment to America much more pleasant than it would have been otherwise." The family looked after him for a year and a half, and Emir, who is in college now, still keeps in touch with them.

He has little doubt that he will be able to return to Bosnia some time in the future. "There's a part of me I left there, and it is missing despite the fact that I've been here for so long and have grown a lot. There is a part of me that doesn't simply exist here, without which I cannot be complete. I hope there is a Bosnia for me to go back to."

Yet Emir knows the life he led as a child in Prijedor is gone. "Most of the non-Serb population in this area has been tortured, raped, or killed by now. The Muslims who have not been killed are homeless and hopeless refugees. They have lost their jobs. Their homes have been burned. Their families are scattered."

When asked whether he would be able to forgive people for what they did, Emir found it difficult to answer. "Who am I to say 'I forgive you?' I can forgive many people, but I deeply believe many things should not be forgiven—at least, not forgotten." For example, "I know people who lost their parents—a terrible loss. I don't know if they could forgive. I would be willing to forgive many people provided they are punished according to the law. . . . If a person killed ten people, he should be tried before a criminal court. The problem is that we probably don't have enough jails."

When asked about his feelings, Emir admitted, "I never tried to examine them. I shall say something I told my father. After my mother reached us in Zagreb, we had a walk one day. My father was in rather high spirits, and I was rather depressed. He said, 'Aren't we happy/lucky?' (Happiness and luck are the same word in our language, and its real meaning is a mixture of both.)

"I said, 'Yes, as happy as we can be, knowing that we cannot be happy.' So, I feel as good as a person like me is entitled to feel. I am here in this strange country, with people who are kind to me and take care of me. I am able to pursue my studies. But everyone likes to be at home. My home has been burned and destroyed. I know that one day I shall return to my country and see my people living in freedom."

Emir translated a poem by Iris Kulasic, another Bosnian student, which expresses the mixed feelings of a refugee. Emir thinks that Iris speaks for him and all the other young Bosnians who may not be able to return to their homes.

Memories

There! I have landed like a seed
    carried by the wind.
Only the roots haven't spread yet.
My soul is dying out,
    from a familiar scent, from tree blossoms,
    from my streets, far away am I, separated.
My heart hurts, still bleeding, and still
    I dream of returning.
Sometimes, it seems, I begin
    to forget.
The images fade away
    disappearing from the mind, but
    some gesture, a well-known sign,
    recalls the bitterness of parting.
And I am alone, the winds
    have blown me away.
God! I don't know where I shall end up. . . .
To one side, the remembrances urge me
    onward, but the current will not let me—
I lose sight of you.[2]

Adis

One of the most moving stories of a Good Samaritan was told by Adis, a fifteen-year-old student attending high school in Westchester County, New York.[3] On May 25, 1992, Adis and his mother walked from their hometown, Kozarec (Ko-ZAH-rats), to a nearby village to visit his grandmother. He remembers that day well because it was his thirteenth birthday and also the day Serbian forces attacked.

At first, Adis's father and sister, Alisa, assumed that Adis and his mother had been killed in the attack. But they weren't dead. They had walked to the next village, Trnopolje (TURN-o-pol-ye), where Muslims were being rounded up to be placed in a concentration camp. "We were put into the camp," he said. "From the camp you could either be sent to Omarska, known as a death camp, or released as a refugee in central Bosnia."

Adis was imprisoned at the camp for one and a half months. It was not long before his father and sister were among the Muslims rounded up and brought there, along with his uncle and grandmother. The uncle had been tortured and starved for twenty days at Omarska, losing about sixty-five pounds. Adis said, "I was forced to watch people being beaten, but didn't see anyone killed. Then we were forced out of the camp, to watch Muslim houses being burned. Our house was also burned down, but we didn't see it."

The detention center that Adis remembers was for women and children. "It was simply a school building and an adjacent gym, surrounded by barbed wire and a minefield. We were given one meal a day. It was warm water, with salt and a little rice." When the building became too crowded, "the women and children were moved to nearby Muslim apartments that had been emptied out." Now in the United States, he said, "it is hard for me to live with these memories. I have bad dreams and nightmares."

Then something strange happened to Adis's mother. "Years before she had set up a knitting factory for abused women. She had no job for one woman who applied and [the woman] then began to cry. My mother asked her what was the matter. The woman needed money to buy

51

books, so she could go to school. My mother opened her purse and gave her the money."

Later, a Serb guard at the camp appeared in an armored car with orders to take Adis's mother to Omarska. "Do you know where I'm taking you?" he asked her. "It's a place from which people don't come back alive." Then he explained to her that he was the brother of the woman whom she had helped years ago. "I will protect you," he told her, "and take you where you'll be safe."

Adis's mother could not go back to her home, so they decided her best chance for survival was to return to the camp. The guard provided her with a fake ID as just an ordinary prisoner, which would make her eligible for release to a nearby village. Eventually, after six months the whole family was reunited there, and the guard took them all in his armored car to Prijedor to stay with relatives. Throughout this time, he brought them food and—even more precious to them—words of encouragement.

The special good deed of Adis's mother had earned her the respect of this Serb soldier, who repaid it. Even though Adis has a sad expression when he smiles in his new home, he sounds hopeful. "I need to finish my education," he said, "and go back to Bosnia when the war is over." What stands out for him is "the Serb soldier who saved my mother's life."

In April 1994, he heard the news: "I would come to America. I wasn't very happy at first," because it would mean "leaving my friends and my family." But his older sister, Alisa, had gone ahead, to Exeter, Massachusetts, and she helped arrange the invitation for Adis. His hosts

Adis found out in April 1994 that he would be able to come to the United States. He joined his sister, Alisa, (right) who had already come to America.

in the United States wrote to him, as his foster father recalled, "We're not a very wealthy family, but we would love to have you." They had heard about Adis through their church in Westchester County.

The letters and pictures that he received made Adis feel better about the chance to continue his education at a good school. His hosts had arranged for a scholarship from a Catholic school, Iona Prep. The first time Adis filled out the forms at the United States embassy in Zagreb, he was turned down. "I wasn't fluent in English. I had to get a new invitation from Iona," which spelled out that he could learn the language there. A few months later, he finally got his student visa.

Now, Adis seems at home with the son and daughter of his host family. He is happy at school with a full schedule of "physical science, biology, math, English, and religion." He doesn't mind going to chapel at school, as he is not made to say the prayers, and he said, "I'm not very religious" as a Muslim. At the time of his interview, Adis had been in the United States only a month. He spends a good deal of time at home, playing with the family's two dogs. But in school he has "found one Croatian student who speaks my language, and he has very nice parents who invite me to visit."

Adis clearly misses his parents, who are still refugees in Croatia, and other relatives who are scattered thoughout Germany and Sweden. His one link to the family is his sister, Alisa, who is planning to transfer to a school closer to her brother. He is not sure, however, when, or if, he will be able to see the rest of the family again.

Lejla

Lejla is a twenty-three-year-old woman from Mostar who is also haunted by bad memories of the war.[4] She has long blond hair and hazel eyes, and she expresses herself clearly in English, in a strong, determined voice.

Lejla's nightmares bring back "the fifteen days I had to spend in an atomic bomb shelter, with my sister, my parents, and friends. It was so cold. We were playing cards, with only candles for light. They had turned off the electricity. We had taken a couple of candles, but we couldn't sleep. Every bed had only one blanket.

"What was interesting was that some Serbs were there with us, too. A good friend of mine was a Serbian whose older brother was at the entrance to the shelter with a gun, taking care of us. I thought we were hiding from the Serbian army, but he thought that *they* were hiding from the Croats! It was so confusing. . . . My Serb friend was telling me the Croats will attack now because it's Christmas and they want revenge."

The actual fighting didn't break out until much later. In the meantime, Lejla and her younger sister were sent to safety in Zagreb. Their father came to visit them. "But on his way back home he was arrested. When he hadn't arrived home, I called an uncle and told him my father was missing. My uncle checked all the prisons in the area, and he found him.

"When my uncle talked to the Serbian soldiers, they refused to release my father. They said it was against the rules to let him go. Then my uncle told the soldier in charge of the prison who my father was. The soldier said, 'Why didn't you say so before? I didn't know he was here. He's a good friend of mine. We played football for twenty-five years together.' When they took my father out, he didn't know what was going on.'"

Fortunately, Lejla's father had only been kept in a locked cell for seven days; he had not been tortured. He was able to get back to Mostar, where he and his wife "still live in the basement of their house. When there is nothing left but to survive, then you do." The Serbian army surrounding Mostar has cut off the phones and electricity, so Lejla can talk to her parents only rarely. Her father, she said, "is still optimistic that this is going to end, but it doesn't."

Like other Muslim refugees in Zagreb, Lejla and her sister found it difficult to find a place to live that they could afford. "We were living with ten other people in a small apartment, and I had to find a job." If you are persistent you can find a menial job in a restaurant, she said. As Muslims, she and her sister couldn't go to school.

Lejla joined some of the students she knew from Mostar and Sarajevo, where she had attended the university, to organize an association of Bosnian students. They found a tiny room to meet in and to "send out letters to more and more people asking them to help us." When Sheikh Tosun Bayrak of the Jerrahi Order came to visit them, "we didn't have chairs. We were all sitting on the floor."

But the Sheikh was impressed by the spirit and organization of the students. "He said they could take my sister and find her a high school to attend in the United States. I said, 'But I can't just leave her.' And the Sheikh said, 'All right, we'll find you a scholarship, too!' That was it!"

Like many of the Bosnian students, Lejla has been getting honor grades at Iona College, and she is going to graduate school next year, probably at the University of Missouri. Her uncle and aunt, who have come as refugees, will be nearby, in St. Louis. And her parents "have all the necessary papers to come over, but so far they haven't been given their visas." American officials can grant or deny permission based on their impression of applicants—in this case on whether or not they have the skills to find work.

Despite her upbeat tone and academic success, Lejla is anxious about her future. "There is no place to go back to. Everything has been taken over by the Serbs." She said, "It is especially hard for people in mixed marriages," like her parents. She wonders if it will ever be possible to find once more "the spirit of Sarajevo—the breath of the city" that made people of all ethnic backgrounds feel at home.

Suljo

Suljo explained his name is short for Sulejman. "That's a Muslim name, quite common, but you can't succeed with that name in Bosanski Petrovac [BOSS-ahn-skee PET-ro-vats]."[5] The population of his hometown was about fifteen thousand, 80 percent Serb and 20 percent Muslim. Of the Muslims, he says, "thousands were killed, two hundred of them in the first two days of the war, my best friends among them."

Like most of the Bosnian students, Suljo is still in shock about the sudden end to his prewar life, and he is searching for answers. "Before the war my family had a nice life. We had everything we needed: a car, a house, and so on. In school, I was always in first place. But overnight we lost everything my parents had worked for [for] twenty years."

How did it happen? He said, "There was a Serb-approved mythology that encouraged the killing of Muslims." Suljo was referring to the spreading of stories that led to the belief that Muslims were a threat to their Christian neighbors. He had not been aware of it until "the military and our neighbors forced all Muslims to leave. Our houses were promised to Serbs who had come to serve [in the army]. . . . The Serbs wanted to kill all Muslims or force them out of Bosnia, just as Spain did to the Jews in the fifteenth century."

For Suljo, an honors student in his high school who had begun attending the University of Sarajevo, Serb threats quickly led to the forced removal of his family. "Big trucks took us away," he said, "and we heard sniper shooting."

He recalled, "They killed ten people in the truck. I spent seven hours scrunched up."

His family made it to safety in Slovenia, then a year later they became refugees in Croatia. There his father, "a skilled bus driver, couldn't work. We only received humanitarian aid," said Suljo. "I feel responsible for my family."

Since his family became divided, however, there has been little Suljo has been able to do for them. Eventually, his parents and younger sister "were able to go to Italy for a better life." Suljo himself "went to Turkey but wasn't allowed to go to college." Then the Bosnian Student Project found him "a scholarship to West Chester University, in Pennsylvania. . . . My only wish is to finish school and be a success. I am still young and can regain my hope, but I am very unhappy for my parents. All their hope is in me."

Suljo said, "I talk to my parents every two weeks." They often talk about their homeland, Bosnia, where he would like to "be an engineer" and help repair the destruction of war. He said, "Bosnians need help from the West to make a stable country with human rights for everybody." But then he is shocked to discover that in the United States, "many people have no idea where Bosnia is."

Suljo expressed hope for the future, but his memories turn up in his nightmares. For example, he said, "I dream that people are getting killed and not even my Serb best friend would help." He recognizes that this is close to the truth: "Nobody wants to help Bosnia."

4

Growing Up and Taking Charge

Those who have experienced the terror and uncertainty of war often express surprise at how quickly they left childhood behind and took charge of their own lives. Some of the students were sent away by their parents to towns and cities in Bosnia that were supposed to be safe, but were soon attacked by Serbian or Croatian armies. Others escaped with one or both parents to Zagreb, Croatia's capital. While there was no fighting in Zagreb, there was also no legal way for their parents to earn money because Bosnian Muslims were considered foreigners. The Bosnian students discovered that Croatian schools were closed to them as well. Although the Bosnians started up schools of their own, there was no money to pay the teachers, and few books and supplies.

As refugees, the Bosnians were dependent upon the charity of friends and relatives for housing, and on international relief organizations for food. Some of the older students or their parents helped to distribute food and clothing for these organizations. Others, especially those who knew English, went to the refugee camps with the United Nations Human Rights Commission to help translate the stories of those who had been in concentration camps. In that way, they earned money.

When the students interviewed for this book arrived in the United States, their feelings of loss and separation often intensified. Still, they were relieved to be allowed to live a relatively normal life while attending high school or college. Being on their own as young adults in a foreign country has not always been easy.

Edin

Edin was fourteen years old when the war began in his hometown of Brcko (BURTCH-ko).[1] He was sent to live with his aunt in the nearby city of Tuzla (TOOZ-lah), where his parents thought he would be safe. His father, an engineer, became the first commander of the Bosnian resistance. His mother, a lab technician, was quickly pressed into service as a nurse.

"The Serbs needed my city," Edin said, "because they needed a corridor to get from their part of Bosnia to other areas, and we were strategic."

The mountains surrounding Tuzla were soon filled with Serb soldiers who rained down a constant barrage of mortar and machine-gun fire on the civilians.

"My mom thought she could protect me. She kept

61

The damage to a mosque in the town of Brcko is evident in this photo. Brcko is located directly in the Serbians' path to other parts of Bosnia.

phoning, and forbade me to go out of the apartment because of the shelling in the town.

"The worst thing was that I didn't care. The worst thing is when you don't have a survival instinct. You sort of let yourself go. 'If it hits me, it hits me.' That's what you think. And that doesn't come consciously. It just comes. It is your way of saying, 'No, I won't let *you* ruin my life. I can have just that little control over my life. I can go anywhere I want."

Of course, Edin admitted, "this is very risky because the mortar shell can hit you anytime—anytime, when you are out walking or when you are in the apartment."

The war affected Edin in many different ways. There were things he never thought about before the war, such as "which mountain had the highest peak, or what apartment is in the best position, and how thick are the walls. During a war you don't sleep in the bedroom. You sleep in the hallways. So if a mortar shell hits, it will hit the walls, but it can't get to you."

Before the war, Edin always slept soundly. Now he slept "like a cat. And the mortar shells—by the second month you knew the sound. It sort of goes 'puff' and you have exactly three seconds to get out. If it whistles, it is not going to hit your area. But if you don't hear it, it will hit you. Knowing this is a matter of life and death.

"The weird thing is that you feel as if you are living through a dream, and you want it to end. So sometimes you are very jolly, or sometimes you are very depressed. When there was electricity, I watched television or went out, and tried not to think about the war. Then the news would come on, and there would be no defense.

"And I always thought, there is something worse.

What if I were a refugee? But I was staying with my aunt." Many people were fleeing to Tuzla because it was relatively safe. Although there was constant sniper fire, there was no door-to-door combat.

Edin would walk through the streets and see the stream of refugees every day. They would be given one blanket per person and be sent to the school gym. He would think, "There is always worse than worse. You couldn't think, 'I don't like this, or I'm not satisfied with this accommodation.' The war helps you understand some things. If you have everything granted [to you] you don't have a feeling. If something were taken away from you, then you have an intimate sense of loss.

"Before the war I went to school and went to piano school, which I hated," he said. He did, however, love to play tennis. He would come to appreciate this sport even more later on.

Edin stayed in Tuzla from May 1992 until January 1993. In November 1992, his father left Brcko for Croatia to see if he could get some UN aid—food and medicine—for his town. Edin's mother and older sister, Edina, came to stay with him in Tuzla. "That was a very tough time for us. My father is the one who controlled and master-minded the house. My dad planned for us and made decisions. So when he left, you felt there was no one to guide you."

Edin's mother "literally froze with fear when a mortar attack came," said Edin. "And I would carry her or drag her down the stairs. It's not that she didn't want to go, it's just that she froze. Literally, she was scared stiff. So I would care for her."

When Edin's father finally returned from his mission

to Croatia, he decided that they should all go to Zagreb where they would be safe. They traveled by car over rough mountain roads because the main roads were closed. Their travel was made more difficult because the narrow, twisting roads were clogged with cars filled with people trying to escape the fighting. The two-day ride was full of danger. "There were checkpoints," Edin recalled. "All around the mountains were Serbs." At each checkpoint his father would ask if it were safe to pass. Sometimes there were long waits, and they would talk to others who were fleeing. Many didn't want to leave, others wanted to get away as quickly as possible.

"I have flashes of images that come back to me. My mom was scared, but my sister and I were laughing. I don't know how my father dealt with us, because the three of us were crazy. And you have this whole range of emotions," he said.

Because Edin's father was a commander with the Bosnian resistance he had to be very careful. If the Serbs found him, he would certainly have been killed. Finally, after two harrowing days, the family reached the outskirts of Zagreb, where they stayed for ten days. On the eleventh, they went to the center of the city.

For the first few weeks, Edin's aunt and his uncle—a Croat—put the family up, but soon they were able to move to their own apartment. "I had the feeling that I was a kid again. My father was working, but my mom and my sister and I were together. We snuggled and cuddled together. Even though I was fourteen, it felt so good. I remember Zagreb like that. Not of being free, although I was safe from mortar shells and everything. But I did have the feeling of being loved. It was a gentle feeling."

Sometimes Edin's father's friends would stop by to talk. But there were never any kids around. Finally, Edin learned that one of his friends from elementary school was in Zagreb. "Her name is Edina, like mine (and my sister). We were the best of friends. I went to see her a couple of times. If you are my age or younger, you are just turned upside down. You realize your friend—her father is maybe killing your family in Tuzla. The war—the thing is we never discussed it. I never said to Edina, 'I'm a Muslim.' Nor did she say to me, 'I'm a Serb.' You know your religion forms you as a person, but it doesn't define you as a person."

One day Edin heard the Jerrahi Order was looking for young Bosnians to bring to America so that they could go to school there. Edin was asked if he wanted to apply.

"But I didn't have any hope of being chosen. I figured that they were looking for students who were geniuses. Even though I had always been a straight-A student, I never thought of myself as being smart. But I said I would apply."

Two months later Edin learned that the American Consulate had granted him a visa. "That was the happiest day of my life. But I was happy without thinking that I would have to leave my parents and go into the world by myself. You don't realize these things until you actually go through them. You don't realize what it's like to leave your family and go to school and adapt. Now I think I'm a pretty strong person. One thing that carries me is that I'm one of the few who was given the chance to come, and I will do anything to keep that chance. To be transported from Bosnia to Croatia, and then to fly to

America all in a few months—I don't know what I did in my life to deserve this."

When Edin arrived in the United States, he was met by Sheikh Tosun Bayrak and Jamal Mesalic, a friend of Edin's father. Mesalic came to the United States many years ago. He works for the United Nations Bosnian Mission. He took Edin to live with his family, and almost immediately he felt at home. Mesalic's wife is Bosnian, and "cooks like a Bosnian. Semsa is a great cook," Edin said with a smile.

When school began, Edin was nervous. Although he had studied English in his high school, he felt uneasy speaking it with Americans. He thought, "Am I good enough? I really wanted to be since I was given this chance. I just couldn't let anyone down. It would be an embarrassment not only for me, but I would do anything for my father. I would kill myself for him.

"You know, I always felt that in America it was a good life. Zagreb was a haven, but it didn't give me a new start. But America—it was a new life, a new start."

Edin entered Mt. Olive High School in Flanders, New Jersey. At first he was overwhelmed by the challenges he faced. Unlike his school in Brcko, he was expected to make choices of the courses he would take, and the schedules were so different. "In my country we would have language on Monday and Thursday. Here, you have all subjects every day. And I felt really strange when I had to ask for a pass to go the bathroom. It's not like I'm going to run away or anything like that."

From the start, though, Edin loved his teachers, whom he, like all Bosnians, calls "Professor." "I had a couple of subjects I adored. I'm going to major in business in college, but I'm very interested in art history, so I took art history in my school." He also took American history, calculus, English, accounting, ancient civilization, and advanced computer application.

When Edin discovered that his new school had a tennis team, he immediately tried out and made the team. "This was really something for me. I became number one in tennis. The thing with tennis is that when you play, you really don't think of anything else but tennis. You can't think about the ball and think about your family at the same time."

By the time Edin had completed his junior year in high school, he had done so well that his guardian thought he should skip his senior year and go directly to college.

Mesalic gave Edin the tuition money to attend Morris County Community College. All the while Edin studied at the community college, he worried. "What if I finish here, and can't get a scholarship to a [four-year] college? What will I do? I was on a student visa and I was worried sick." He applied to nearby Ramapo College and waited and worried.

Ramapo College offered him a scholarship. "That was around August 20, 1994, and I had to make up my mind to start school on the fifth of September."

This was a hard moment for Edin. He had to swallow down his emotions, and "say good-bye to the family I learned to love. I was so sad. I didn't want to lose any more people." But once Edin moved into the dormitory and started his classes, he was all right. And at Christmas time he was able to return to his host family for a visit.

Edin wants to finish Ramapo College and go on to graduate school. But he misses his family. "My father

Edin entered high school in New Jersey upon arriving in the United States. He went on to a community college, and later earned a scholarship to a four-year college. While he misses his family very much, he wants to finish college and go on to graduate studies.

goes to Bosnia every ten days and delivers food. And my mother worries. The first couple of times I called, she couldn't talk to me. She just cried. I cried, too. Now, however, it is better." Edin's sister, Edina, has gone to Germany, where she married a fellow Bosnian refugee. At the time of this interview [December 1994], she was expecting her first child. "It is going to be a boy," said Edin with a wide smile that showed his snaggle tooth. But the deep, sad look returns to his dark eyes—"And I won't be able to go to see them."

Most of all, Edin longs to return to Bosnia, and his beloved town of Brcko. "You know, there we pay attention to things like trees. I remember them blossoming, and what they look like in the fall. We Bosnians are very easily satisfied. Americans have the idea that satisfaction is to go somewhere. To us, satisfaction is a tree blossoming. I know it sounds corny, but we really are in love with each tree and flower.

"You know I didn't witness murders. Although I did witness mortar attacks, and I saw people wounded. But I never grew cynical. The best thing was that I kept an open view of everything. During a war you see a lot of evil. You yourself can become part of that evil."

Namik

"I got shot on September 16, 1992, when I was fifteen," said Namik, who before the war loved all sports, especially soccer and basketball.[2] "I was outside, near the army soup kitchen in my town [Breza (BREZ-ah) near Saravejo] when the shelling started. I ran toward my house. On the way I fell and was hit by a mortar shell. I

Edin wants, most of all, to be able to return to his town of Brcko. Here, a bombed-out building in Brcko serves as a grim reminder of the damage that will face those who do eventually return.

don't remember anything. I woke up in the emergency room of the hospital."

By the time his parents found out where he was, Namik had already had part of his leg amputated. "Thirteen people died in that attack." Namik recalled. Another friend had also been hit. Because the hospital was so crowded, the Bosnian government sent Namik and his friend to a hospital in Ankara, Turkey. "Here I had one more operation. I had physical therapy. I was in the hospital for two months and in a rehab center in Turkey for six months more. I began to learn Turkish, but I wanted to go back to Bosnia. I left with two friends, but we got only as far as Split, in Croatia. We couldn't get through because of the fighting between the Croats and Muslims. We stayed in Split for three months."

In all that time, Namik had heard from his parents only once. "I was living in an apartment building that the Bosnian government rented for wounded soldiers on the seaside." But Namik's leg was not healing properly, and the government sent him back to Turkey, this time to a hospital in Istanbul. That was in July 1993. There was yet another operation, and this time Namik's leg was amputated above the knee.

Namik stayed in Istanbul for six more months before he met Sheikh Tosun Bayrak. Professor Bayrak was on one of his frequent trips to Istanbul to consult with other Muslim religious leaders on the Bosnian situation and to visit with the Bosnian refugee students. Often he would make it possible for them to attend schools in Turkey. This time Dr. Bayrak arranged for Namik to come to the United States for a new prosthesis (artificial leg) that would allow him to walk without pain, and to continue his education.

At the time Namik was first interviewed for this book [December 1994], he had been in the United States just two weeks. But already he was speaking English. Some of his story was told through a translator. A few weeks later Namik entered Columbia Presbyterian Hospital in New York City, where he was fitted with a prosthesis that allowed him to walk almost normally. Then he traveled to Olympia, Washington, to live with Brian and Mary Baird, and to complete his high school education.

Barely six months after Namik moved to Washington, he was speaking fluent English. And with his new artificial leg he is able to take part in sports again. His host family loves skiing and rock climbing and have taught Namik both sports.

During his first summer in America, Namik attended an advanced class in English as a second language (ESL) at the local community college. He was a high school junior when school resumed in the fall.

What is most difficult for Namik is that he only rarely has contact with his parents, who still live in Breza. Because the town is constantly under attack, Namik has found it very difficult to get through to them either by phone or mail.

Taida

Taida Horozovic is a petite seventeen-year-old girl, barely five feet tall, with large hazel eyes and pale skin[3] "Before the war," she said, "I had a nice life in Banja Luka. There were no worries. My life was nice and . . . 'pink,'

Namik is shown here skiing in Washington State in the winter of 1995.

you could say. And in school you could never recognize who is what. We were all the same."

Taida's parents were both writers—her mother a poet and her father editor of a newspaper and author of over thirty books. When the war began, both parents lost their jobs. "And there was this man [a Serb] who had gone to school with my father. And you know, it's just amazing. He began to say all kinds of terrible things about my father on television. And here I had a book that was signed by him to me. It was just horrible. I started crying.

"My parents weren't into material things, so when we lost our apartment, we said 'Well, why shed tears over material things?' What was horrible was to see people being taken away in vans. People were raped and killed in my city."

Taida's parents fled to Zagreb. Taida was sent to study in Turkey because she wasn't permitted to attend school in Croatia. Although she had traveled with her parents to many different countries, her experience in a Turkish boarding school taught her something she hadn't developed before: patience. She said, "We didn't get the understanding we needed, although it wasn't out of meanness. It's just that they [the Turkish teachers] are in a different world.

"But we were in our room twelve hours a day, and it was hard just to stare at the walls and not go crazy. We got up at 7:00, got dressed, and studied for forty-five minutes. Then we'd have breakfast and go to school. After school, we were locked in our dormitory for another forty-five minutes. For thirty minutes we were allowed to walk around in a closed courtyard. Then we would study or write letters from 5:00 to 6:30, have dinner, and then we could run around the courtyard again for thirty minutes. From 8:00 in the evening until 10:30, we were locked in our rooms! At least there were other Bosnian students, and I could talk to them."

In addition to patience, Taida learned "some kind of discipline, and not to always express my feelings." She saved those feelings for her poetry.

Fortunately, Professor Bayrak came to visit Taida's school on one of his periodic trips to Turkey. When he had completed his work there, he traveled to Zagreb and met with Taida's parents, who agreed to let her come to the United States. At the time Taida was interviewed [December, 1994] she was a sophomore in high school, and was living with a Jerrahi host family in Chestnut Ridge, New York. Here is a poem she has written.

A Prayer to Existence

Silent scream of my soul and stars I
    used to watch for such a long time.
In each of those stars one of my dreams
    stood and the sky was the smile of my
    soul watching its reflection in the sea.
And then the dark came along, and all the
    stars became stones that were falling
    on me.
The sky became an angry beast trying to
    steal my soul away.
The sea cried with me.
I closed my eyes to look into myself,
    and falling through the branches of
    conscience, I looked for myself searching
    dusty corners of my mind, desperately

trying to find the way out of that labyrinth that
imprisoned me!
Do you know what it's like, when you have to
murder your own dreams?
Do you know what it's like when you
have to feed your own pain and fear so
it would make you want to struggle and
survive another day?

5

Hope for the Future

Soon after Bosnia declared its independence and the war began in April 1992, the college students who were attending the university in Zagreb were stranded. They couldn't get back to their families in Bosnia because many of the roads were blocked. The university made them leave their dormitory rooms, took away their meal tickets, and dismissed them from the school because Bosnians were now considered to be foreigners, no longer entitled to a free education. The only way back to the university was to pay the very high fees charged to foreign students. Moreover, Bosnians were forbidden to work legally. Cut off from their families, unable to finish their studies, the students soon ran out of money. Some were able to find odd jobs that the government could not find out about from Croatian friends. Other

Croatian students offered their Bosnian friends a place to sleep. Some Bosnian students lived in the streets, sleeping in parks or in empty buildings. Added to the daily worry of finding enough to eat, a place to sleep, and avoiding the authorities, many students were unable to contact their parents, and feared they were dead.

Despite these hardships, several students decided to speak to the education ministers to see what, if anything, could be done. When they didn't get any help from government officials, they decided to organize themselves, and see if there was anyone in the world who was willing to help them.

Damir

"Seven days before the war began in my town of Kozerac (ko-ZAH-rats), which is near Banja Luka, my mother had a strange feeling," said Damir, who was then a senior at the University of Zagreb.[1] "She sent my brother, Zlatan who was just fourteen, to Zagreb."

For the next two months—from May to July 1992—neither Damir nor Zlatan knew if their parents were alive or dead. "We knew that Serbs were in our town, and we knew what could happen. To add to their worries, he had very little money. Damir arranged for his brother to live with friends, while he slept in a car or on the streets. Finally, he found a place to share with others, but he had only enough money for two months rent.

Meanwhile, Damir's parents, along with hundreds of other Muslims, had been taken to Trnopolje (TURN-o-pol-ye), a concentration camp. "But one Serb helped them escape. In that camp was another family with a

79

small girl, and my mother was this little girl's teacher. This Serb was a friend of theirs. When the Serb came to help that family, the little girl said, 'I don't want to get out without my teacher.' And it was a miracle. They were really lucky, because that Serb said, 'O.K. Get into the car, and I'll take you out!'"

For the next several months Damir's parents went into hiding. Finally a representative of the International Red Cross helped his parents cross over into Croatia.

Damir and his parents had no way to contact each other. Luckily, they had each called the same friend in Germany, hoping the other would do the same. One day Damir learned his parents were safe and soon would arrive in Zagreb.

"My brother went every day for two months to the railroad station to wait for the convoys from Bosnia. And then one day we saw our parents."

Their life became more normal, but since his family's bank accounts had been frozen in Bosnia, they were all without money. Damir still had to fend for himself.

"I was studying economics," said Damir. "But when something happened between the Bosnian Croats and Bosnian Muslims, my friends and I decided to do something for Bosnian students, and little by little we formed the Bosnian Student Association."

At first a Croatian friend gave them a tiny office. It became a place for students to go for information and friendship. "We organized some programs and got money from the Soros Foundation. [George Soros is a very wealthy businessperson who is known for helping university students in countries that were once under Communist rule.] I was able to finish my senior year in

Zagreb because of Mr. Soros. But I have yet to get my diploma. I have only a piece of paper that says I finished my courses. The head of the university wouldn't give me a real diploma unless I paid them one thousand German marks. One thousand marks! We had better use for that kind of money."

Gradually, the students made connections with various humanitarian organizations in Europe. "We made some deals, and one organization paid each student who was registered with us one hundred fifty or two hundred German marks a month just to buy food. I was really happy to do something for the students. I just felt it was my obligation. I hadn't been in the army. It was my way and the way of my friends to do something for Bosnia," Damir said.

Once the Bosnian Student Association was under way, Damir sent his own transcripts to Doug Hostetter, "and FOR found a scholarship for me."

Damir arrived in New York on December 28, 1993, and was admitted to Butler University in January 1994.

Damir worried about his younger brother, Zlatan, who finished his second year of high school in Croatia, but couldn't continue to study there. With the help of the Jerrahis, Zlatan was able to go to Izmir, Turkey, for a year.

"I was here in the United States, he was in Turkey, and my parents were in Croatia. I wanted to bring him closer to me. It would be easier on my parents to have two sons in one place."

Damir's original host family, the Hostetters, had relatives in Denver, Colorado, who offered to send papers to get Zlatan to America. Zlatan arrived in

Author Harvey Fireside interviewed Damir (shown here) in December 1994.

August 1994, and graduated from South Denver High School on June 4, 1995.

Damir is very proud of his younger brother, who now attends college in New York State. "It was so difficult for him—first year of high school in Bosnia, second in Croatia, third in Turkey, where, when he arrived he knew only twenty words of Turkish, and fourth in Denver. Now my little brother knows English, Turkish and German.

"I miss my parents, my food, my friends and relatives. I miss the time that I lost," Damir said. "I'm sure that one day we'll have our Bosnia again. You know, in Croatia, there are many students in refugee camps who cannot finish their education. When I think about this I could cry. But I learned from a research paper I did that worldwide, 80 percent of the refugees go home after a war. If 80 percent of the Bosnians get back, we can rebuild a new country. I would like to be part of that."

Samir

"I was a student in Croatia for six years," said Samir, who arrived in the United States in March 1994.[2] He stayed in Nyack, New York, with the international secretary of FOR, Doug Hostetter, and his wife, Bobbie, for several months before he went to Cornell University as a graduate student. On the very night he arrived in New York, after having traveled for twenty-four hours on end, Samir sat down at the piano and played and sang Bosnian songs for his host family and their friends who had come to welcome him.

"America is many different things," Samir discovered. "It is one way when you look at it from

Samir sat down at the piano to play some Bosnian music upon arriving at his host family's home in Nyack, New York.

Europe, and another when you see America and you are here. I came with the old eyes from Europe. America is a country above all countries. Living in America is something special. But, you know, in our country we had cars, we had apartments. Of course, people in America have a lot more stuff, and the standard of living is higher. But nothing was strange for me."

What has startled Samir most is that people criticize the government constantly. "Democracy in America is much ahead of other democracies. Sometimes when I watch TV, I think that people didn't vote for their own government the way people criticize it." Democracy is something Samir admires very much.

Samir, along with Damir and others, was one of the organizers of the students in Zagreb. "I had just completed my undergraduate degree in civil engineering when the war started," he recalled. "I was planning on going somewhere in Europe for awhile, but I always wanted to come back to Bihac." Samir's family has been in Bihac for countless generations. You can hardly go anywhere in his city without meeting one of his relatives. But the last time he saw his family was in 1992 when he went home to vote on whether or not Bosnia should become a separate country. "This meant that we would be in a country of Serbs and Croats and Muslims and Jews," he said. His belief that Bosnia was and should be multi-ethnic and multicultural is unshakable.

The war began shortly after he returned to Zagreb. The situation became very confused, because the Muslims and Croats began to fight each other, too. "Many Muslims had to leave Croatia. Muslim students were being picked up and exchanged for Croatian prisoners of war. It was a hard time. But for me, actually, nothing happened. I knew Zagreb like my own town, and I had Croatian friends. They helped me and gave me money and a place to live, even though there was fighting between Muslims and Croats."

Because Samir had received a college degree and had time, he took a leadership role in the Bosnian Student Association along with several others.

Gradually, as word of their situation got out, some organizations offered help. "We got some money from the World University Service in Austria. Professor Wolfgang Benedek from Graz, a professor of international studies got us a computer, and the Jerrahis gave us money. Many students were able to go to Austria. That is because the Queen of Austria, Queen Maria Theresa, left money for all students who were once part of the Austro-Hungarian empire. And the former Yugoslavia was once part of that empire. We had researched this and found out that many of our students qualified!"

When Samir first came to America he helped out in the FOR office while he studied to improve his English. It is not a language that comes easily to him. Little by little, he met people whom he can call his friends. "You make your nest, your network and connections, and that is what makes your life for us who are out of our homes. I feel safe here, and connected. At least I can call somebody up and ask some questions. But in the beginning, it is hard.

"The most important thing here at Cornell is the faculty. They offer to help the students, and there is a much better relationship between the faculty and students than in my country. But during the first semester I had to accustom myself to a new culture and to new technology. And also, my English still wasn't so good."

Samir also worried about his family in Bihac. "My city was constantly under attack. There was no food there, and no humanitarian aid could get through. My mother, father, my brother and sister are all there. I had one first cousin killed, one second cousin killed, some neighbors were killed, and other friends from my youth were killed. So each time I call my family, I am afraid that I will hear that someone else got killed or wounded. And people are dying not only because of starvation and not only because of shootings, they are just dying.

"The worst thing for us is that we are helpless. We can't send them [our families] anything, and we have been unable to change the minds of the United Nations or America or Europe to change their policy towards our country. And we don't understand why somebody wants to kill us without reason. What is the reason they are killing us? Why does the world let them do that? This is something I can't understand."

During the entire month before Christmas 1994, while Samir was studying hard for his final exams, the Serbs bombed Bihac virtually every day. No one could contact the people inside the city. Samir did not know if his family was still alive. Finally, on the day after Christmas, Samir decided to make one more effort to phone his family. He finally got through to them at 3 A.M. (9 A.M. in Bihac). In order to do this, he had to call a mobile phone operator at a post office in Zagreb. That person called the family from another phone. When the

The remains of the bombed-out buildings of Krupa, near Bihac, are shown here. Two men are helping to fix the roof of the building on the left.

contact was made, the operator held two phones receiver-to-receiver, and for a few minutes, Samir and his parents could talk. "It is very hard. And because it is a mobile phone, and works on the radio, everyone can listen in," said Samir. "The Serbs can listen in and jam the connections." Still, it was the first time in over a month that Samir heard his parents' voices. It was the best Christmas present he could have had.

The second semester went more easily for Samir, though he still had trouble with English. At the end of the second semester, he got a paid internship with the Department of Water and Sewers in the town of Ithaca. "I've been designing some roads and dams and bridges. I'm involved with a lot of different projects, and this is all in my field. I'm getting excellent work experience."

Sometimes Samir can have some fun. "I can have a good time watching a movie, and I go to parties and receptions. I've made friends with other students, but, you know, students live very busy lives."

Samir is aware that once he has earned his graduate degree in engineering, he will have to make a decision about where he will go. Except for one or two cousins, Samir is the only one in his family who has left Bihac, and, he has said, he would be happy to return there to help rebuild it.

"I like that I have the opportunity to study here, and I think that it is very good for me, and my family, and my country. I like the way the people in the Bosnian Student Project have helped me, because I didn't just get a fish. I got the fishing pole, as well."

Samir has given a great deal of thought to the war in Bosnia. "I think that this war is very similar to the second World War, when one country invaded another. What we have in Bosnia is genocide. It is fascism. Bosnians in Bosnia were made up of Muslims, Croats, Serbs, and Jews. The genocide is against the Muslims in Bosnia. I don't know why the international community has allowed this to happen. Is this because we are a country without oil, or because we are Muslims who are secular from Europe, with white skin and light eyes? Or is it just because nobody cares about us? I think in the end someone will have to do something, because this war could extend out of Bosnia to Macedonia and Bulgaria and other countries. You know the Muslims from Bosnia are Slavic people, just like Croats and Serbs. We were all Bosnians together within our borders. I hope that people in the international community will realize that we want to live together in a country with equal opportunities, regardless of religion and nationality. We are not nationalistic. Our flag has as its symbol a lily—it is a symbol of peace."

Conclusion:
Going Home—
A Dream of Reality

On November 21, 1995, the presidents of Serbia, Croatia, and Bosnia agreed to end the four-year-old war among the Croats, Muslims, and Serbs in Bosnia. This treaty is known as the Dayton Accords, because the three warring parties met in Dayton, Ohio.

Bosnia was divided into two parts, a Muslim-Croat federation and a Serb republic. All three parties are to share a central law-making body and presidency. Sarajevo will be the capital. The Muslim-Croat federation would have 51 percent of Bosnia, the Serb republic, 49 percent.

To make sure the shooting will end, an armed peace-keeping force of sixty thousand troops would be sent to Bosnia under the North Atlantic Treaty Organization (NATO). About twenty thousand of these troops are

American. Other countries who agreed to send troops are France, England, Russia, and Belgium.

Before the war all of the cities in Bosnia were open to Muslims, Croats, and Serbs. Now some cities are designated Serbian, while others will belong to the Muslim-Croat federation. The Serbs wanted certain Bosnian cities because they were a link to Serbia. The Serbs gained the cities of Zepa and Srebrenica, even though before the war both had been largely Muslim. The Serbs also gained Banja Luka, Brcko, and Pale. The Muslim-Croat federation will control a five-mile-wide corridor that links Sarajevo and Gorazde. Bosnian Serbs had to give up control of the neighborhoods and suburbs surrounding Sarajevo so that the city could be unified. Other cities, such as Bihac, Mostar, Tuzla, and Gorazde, remain part of the Muslim-Croat federation.

The students are very wary of the Dayton treaty. They point out that while the Serbs had fought against both the Muslims and the Croats, the Croats had also fought fierce battles against the Muslims, especially in the city of Mostar. They are concerned that the Croats may start fighting the Muslims once the NATO forces leave Bosnia.

The Dayton peace treaty recognizes that there are nearly 3 million refugees—Croats, Muslims, and Serbs—who have been driven from their homes. All refugees are supposed to have the right either to return to their homes or to receive payment for lost land and property. A special human rights commission has been appointed to make certain that the refugees are treated fairly. But so far there is no way to make certain that the rights of refugees will be observed. Indeed, even those

A group of students and their sponsors from the Bosnian Student Project meet at a local coffee shop in Ithaca, New York. Many of these students are still uncertain if they will ever be able to return to their homes in Bosnia.

students who are from cities that remain in the hands of Muslims, know that their family homes have been completely destroyed. Students whose cities are now in the hands of the Serbs wonder just where they will be able to live. Those from mixed marriages—Serb-Muslim or Croat-Muslim—feel "ethnic cleansing" forever destroyed their dream of a multicultural society for them and their parents in Bosnia.

Several students, such as Damir, have returned to visit their parents now living as refugees in Zagreb, Croatia. Damir had not seen his parents in over two years. Since they were forced from Kozerac, they will not be allowed to return to that city. However, Damir's father has been making plans for the future. He makes weekly trips to Bihac, visiting the parents of Samir, and bringing in food and other supplies to sell. He is trying to figure out a way for the two families to go into business together—and perhaps one day there will be a way for Damir and Samir to work together, as well.

It is difficult for most of the students to think about going back to Bosnia just yet. But the suffering of the fellow Bosnians is never far from their thoughts. Maja, who is studying psychology at Cornell University, was awarded a special grant to travel to Croatia where there are several orphanages filled with children known as "rape babies."

Thousands of Muslim women and girls were raped and made pregnant by Serb soldiers. Many of the women were ashamed to tell their families, and when their babies were born, left them in orphanages. In addition to her work with the rape babies, Maja also plans to attend the war crimes trials which will be held in the

Maja, shown here in a reflective moment, will be travelling to Croatia to study the children in orphanages there.

Hague in Holland in 1996. She hopes her English is good enough to get her a position as a translator.

Some steps are being taken by the Fellowship of Reconciliation Bosnian Student Project to help rebuild homes and schools in Bosnia, and to help Muslims, Croats, and Serbs find ways to work together. Small groups of Americans made plans to go to Bosnia with some of the students in the summer of 1996. They plan to expand their program and work on larger projects.

"Many students are making plans to return to Bosnia," says Doug Hostetter, director of the Bosnian Student Project. "But the Bosnian government will have to decide where they can go. There will have to be some sort of authorized resettlement plan for the refugees, and that is not yet in place."

In the meantime, the Bosnian students continue their studies in the United States, and prepare themselves to return to rebuild their country.

Questions for Discussion

There are no absolute solutions to the conflict in Bosnia, but here are ten questions for you to think about.

1. Under what conditions might it be possible for Muslims, Serbs, and Croats to live together once again peacefully in Bosnia?

2. In what ways could each of the Bosnian ethnic groups make amends for injuries it has done to others, including the lives, homes, and property that have been taken?

3. What are some ways in which the past culture of Bosnia, including its mosques, libraries, and museums, could be rebuilt?

4. How could the UN or some other outside force identify Serbians, Croats, or Muslims, who have committed "war crimes" and bring those people to justice?

5. If the leaders of the warring groups in Bosnia were chosen because of their ultranationalist platforms, how could they be persuaded to change their views, or how might they be replaced by new leaders?

6. Since there was little or no tradition in Yugoslavia of protecting minority rights by law, how could you ensure that such tolerance is practiced in the future?

7. What might the United States or West European countries do to bring food and medical supplies to the Muslims in the besieged cities, without adding to the violence?

8. Which aspects of the Bosnian conflict have parallels in the United States, in terms of stereotypes of people who tend to become objects of violence?

9. What are some of the basic beliefs of Islam (for example, regarding the sanctity of life), and how do they differ from or resemble those of Christianity and Judaism?

10. How could you, by yourself or with friends, learn more about Bosnia and do something to express your concern?

Chapter Notes

Chapter 1

1. Doug Hostetter, "Scholarships for Bosnian Students," *Fellowship*, November/December 1993, p. 11.

2. Ivan Siber, "The Impact of Nationalism, Values, and Ideological Orientations on Multi-Party Elections in Croatia" in Jim Seroka and Vukasin Pavlovic, eds., *The Tragedy of Yugoslavia: The Failure of Democratic Transformation* (Armonk, N.Y.: M.E. Sharpe, 1992), p. 149.

3. Brian Hall, *The Impossible Country* (Boston: Godine, 1994), p. 14.

4. Misha Glenny, *The Fall of Yugoslavia: The Third Balkan War* (New York: Penguin, 1994), p. 123.

5. Milan Milosevic, "The Media Wars," in Jasminka Udovicki and James Ridgeway, eds., *Yugoslavia's Ethnic Nightmare: The Inside Story of Europe's Unfolding Ordeal* (New York: Lawrence Hill, 1995), p. 113.

6. Stipe Sikavica, "The Collapse of Tito's Army," in Udovicki and Ridgeway, pp. 144–145.

7. *The Europa World Year Book*, "Bosnia," vol. I (London: Europa Publications, 1994), p 567.

8. Sikavica, p. 144.

9. Robert D. Kaplan, *Balkan Ghosts: A Journey through History* (New York: Vintage, 1993), pp. 35–40.

10. Glenny, p. 140.

11. Glenny, pp. 154–155.

12. Ejub Sitkovac and Jasminka Udovicki, "Bosnia and Hercegovina: The Second War," in Udovicki and Ridgeway, p. 190.

13. Lenard J. Cohen, *Broken Bonds: The Disintegration of Yugoslavia* (Boulder, Colo.: Westview Press, 1993), p. 52.

14. Warren Zimmerman, "The Last Ambassador: A Memoir of the Collapse of Yugoslavia," *Foreign Affairs,* March/April 1995, p. 3.

15. Glenny, p. 149.

16. Sabrina P. Ramet, *Nationalism and Federalism in Yugoslavia, 1962–1991* (Bloomington, Ind.: Indiana University Press, 1992). p. 261.

17. Alexandra Stiglmayer, ed., *Mass Rape: The War Against Women in Bosnia-Herzegovina* (Lincoln, Neb.: University of Nebraska Press, 1994), p. 14.

18. Mirko Tepavac, "Tito's Yugoslavia," in Udovicki and Ridgeway, p. 66.

19. Leslie Holmes, *The End of Communist Power* (New York: Oxford University Press, 1993), p. 2.

20. Ronald Suny, "State, Civil Society and Ethnic Cultural Consolidation in the USSR: Roots of the National Question," in Alexander Dallin and Gail W. Lapidus, eds., *The Soviet System: From Crisis to Collapse* (Boulder, Colo.: Westview Press, 1995), p. 354.

Chapter 2

1. All interview material taken from authors' personal interview with Maja, December 27, 1994.

Chapter 3

1. All interview material taken from authors' personal interview with Emir, December 27, 1994.

2. Poem used with permission of Iris Kulasic.

3. All interview material taken from authors' personal interview with Adis, December 27, 1994.

4. All interview material taken from authors' personal interview with Lejla, December 27, 1994.

5. All interview material taken from authors' personal interview with Suljo, December 27, 1994.

Chapter 4

1. All interview material taken from authors' personal interview with Edin, December 27, 1994.

2. All interview material taken from authors' personal interview with Namik, December 28, 1994.

3. All interview material taken from authors' personal interview with Taida, December 27, 1994.

Chapter 5

1. All interview material taken from authors' personal interview with Damir, December 28, 1994.

2. All interview material taken from authors' personal interview with Samir, July 10, 1995.

Index

L